The Brand New Air Fryer Cookbook

Superb Air Fryer Recipes For Beginners And Intermediate Cooks

Sarah Milton

ISBN - 9798849117515

Table of Contents

EXCLUSIVE BONUS

40 Weight Loss Recipes

&

14 Days Meal Plan

Scan the QR-Code and receive
the FREE download:

What is an Air Fryer?

Put simply, an air fryer is a kitchen gadget. It's used to cook your food in a similar way to a traditional convection oven but it is much quicker and more efficient. It's all so much smaller and compact than a built-in oven and can easily be moved around if necessary.

Despite its name, you can use an air fryer to bake, grill, and roast your ingredients. The original air fryer was created and patented by Philips Electronic Company. The patent describes a kitchen appliance that you can use to produce healthier meals than you can by using a deep fryer using only hot air and little to no cooking oil.

Whether you are on a health kick or not, you can benefit from using the air fryer. It produces delicious, crispy foods that you and the whole family can enjoy. We are going to talk more about the benefits of the air fryer later in this book but first, let's take a closer look at how rare fryers work and which foods are best cooked in an air fryer.

How Does an Air Fryer Work?

We won't go too far into the mechanics of the air fryer because that can get pretty complicated! However, let's quickly talk about how an air fryer turns your raw ingredients into a delicious, crispy meal.

A standard air fryer contains several heating elements and a large convection fan that cook your food quickly, evenly, and efficiently. The heating elements provide the necessary hot temperatures to cook the food while the convection farm aid is the movement of hot air around the inner compartment of the machine.

The inside of your air fryer machine will have a mesh basket, in which you place all of your ingredients. When you shut the lid of the air fryer, the heating elements emit very hot air that warms up the inside compartment of the machine. Slowly, this begins to cook your food.

Most air fryer machines can reach temperatures between 180 and 250 degrees Celsius and can run for anywhere from 5 minutes to an hour, meaning you can create a wide range of recipes using this handy gadget.

Unlike a deep fryer, an air fryer doesn't require oil to properly cook your food. Instead, it relies on the circulation of hot air using the heating elements and convection fan within the machine.

When you use an oven or frying pan to cook your food, only one side gets cooked unless you flip the ingredients over during the cooking process. With an air fryer, you don't need to turn over your ingredients to ensure your food gets cooked evenly. Because of the different heating elements and convection fan, your food is cooked on all sides without needing any intervention.

Sarah Milton

How Do You Use An Air Fryer?

Depending on the type of air fryer and the manufacturing company that has made it, air fryer machines can vary. Each machine will have different buttons and settings, and it will come with its own instruction manual.

However, there are some general guidelines that you can follow for almost any kind of air fryer. Below, we've listed the key steps to take when you're cooking using an air fryer. If you're unsure how to use your machine after using these steps, make sure to take a look at the instruction manual.

1. Decide which of the delicious recipes in this book you want to try and get all of the necessary ingredients together.

2. Before you start following the recipe, you will need to preheat the air fryer and line the mesh basket with baking paper or oil.

3. Follow the recipe until you're ready to put the food into the air fryer basket. Transfer your ingredients very carefully into the lined mesh basket, being careful not to touch the heating elements or overfill the basket. Always be cautious when using an air fryer. The heating elements can pose a health and safety risk so make sure to carefully transfer your ingredients in and out of the mesh basket.

4. If you want your food to be extra crispy, you can add a small coating of oil to the ingredients before or after placing them in the air fryer.

5. Shut the air fryer lid and choose the correct temperature setting. Many air fryer machines have pre-set cooking times and temperatures to choose from or you can decide your own settings.

6. Once the lid is closed, all you need to do is wait or continue preparing the rest of your meal. When the food is cooked to your desired crispiness, carefully remove it from the mesh basket and serve.

7. Wait for the machine to cool down before cleaning the mesh basket, ready for the next time you want to use the machine.

What Are the Different Types of Air Fryers and Their Unique Benefits and Drawbacks?

There are lots of different kinds of air fryers and the best kind for you depends on your preferences and the kinds of foods that you ai to cook in your air fryer. Consider your budget and preferred style of cooking when choosing the best machine for your needs.

So, what are the main kinds of air fryers that you can get? Here are the three most common kinds of air fryer machines that you can find either in your local kitchen gadgets store or online.

Cylindrical Basket Air Fryers

Traditional air fryers have an inner mesh basket in which you place all of your ingredients. Most of the recipes in this book will tell you to place all of your ingredients in the mesh basket because this kind of air fryer is the most common and the most popular.

This type of air fryer heats your ingredients using several heating elements and a large fan that increases convection and circulates the hot air around the inner compartment of the machine. The mesh baskets are removable so you can easily add and remove your ingredients from the air fryer without burning yourself or spilling anything.

The heating elements usually reach the correct temperature within a few minutes and begin cooking your food quickly and efficiently. Because they're nice and compact, they don't heat your whole kitchen up like a traditional convection oven.

The two main drawbacks of the cylindrical basket air fryers are their size and functionality. Because they're relatively small and compact, they can't hold large amounts of food and tend to have limited functions. Most basket air fryers are only able to cook a certain range of foods at once.

Convection Oven Air Fryers

Convection oven air fryers use the same heating mechanism as the cylindrical basket air fryers. However, they have racks that enable you to separate your foods more easily inside the machine. This is a feature that basket air fryers don't offer.

You can use convection oven air fryers for baking, grilling, frying, roasting, and broiling. It's noise-free and has a higher capacity than basket air fryers, so you can cook larger portions at once. Because the lid or door of the oven air fryer is made out of glass, you can keep track of your food while it's cooking so you don't overcook it.

Paddle Air Fryers

If you prefer stress-free cooking ad you'd rather not spend half of your evening in the kitchen, paddle air fryers are probably the best option for you. Paddle air fryers are perfect when you want to throw your ingredients into the machine and forget about the util they're fully cooked.

With other kinds of air fryers, you need to flip your food over to ensure it cooks evenly. However, with the paddle air fryer, the food is turned automatically on a paddle. Your food is cooked on every side so you can get a deliciously crispy meal.

This type of air fryer is spacious so it's ideal for a range of dishes, including curries, chilis, risottos, and more.

Sarah Milton

Where Can You Buy a Great Air Fryer?

There are lots of different brands that sell air fryers and they are available in a range of in-person and online stores. It might take you a while to find the best air fryer for your needs because they all offer unique settings and benefits, and they're all different prices.

Take a look online to check the ratings and reviews of different air fryers. Make a list of three or four potential options

Consider the features, temperature settings, prices, and potential drawbacks of each option by seeing what previous customers have liked and disliked about them. Check the specifications of each machine that you're considering to determine whether or not it meets your needs and wants.

Eventually, you will find the perfect air fryer machine that has all of the settings that you want for an affordable price.

We know it can be difficult to search through the hundreds of different air fryer brands that are out there. That's why we've created a list of the most popular high-quality brands to consider if you're searching for a great air fryer.

1. Black and Decker Purify Air Fryer

2. Breville Halo Rotisserie Air Fryer Oven

3. Cosori Pro 4.7L Air Fryer

4. Instant Vortex Plus Dual Air Fryer

5. Philips Avance Turbo-Star Air Fryer

6. NINJA Foodi MAX 14-in-1 SmartLid Air Fryer

7. PowerXL Vortex Air Fryer

8. Sage the Smart Oven Air Fryer

9. Tower T17023 Air Fryer

What Are the Best Foods to Cook Using an Air Fryer?

Air fryers are highly versatile. You can cook a wide range of different foods in your machine, from pancakes to stews to meats and veggies. Air fryers are also great for desserts like chocolate pudding, profiteroles, and cheesecakes. No matter what meal or snack you fancy eating, you won't struggle to make exactly what you're craving when you have an air fryer to hand.

When you browse through the recipes in this book, you will notice the huge variance in the different types of meals and foods that are appropriate for the air fryer. Some of the most popular foods to cook in the air fryer include:

- Poultry meats, such as chicken and turkey

- Fish

- Tofu and tempeh

- Eggs

- Vegetables

- Potato wedges and chips

- Cakes and pastries

You can also use your air fryer to defrost foods from the freezer, such as frozen ready meals, burgers, or vegetables.

If you want to use oil in your recipes, we recommend that you use plant-based oil instead of butter to achieve maximum crispiness. All of the recipes in this book will use olive oil but any plant-based oil should be suitable to use in your air fryer machine.

Additional Benefits of Using an Air Fryer

Air fryers provide a wide range of benefits. Some of the key benefits include:

1. Little to no oil is required to cook food in the air fryer, so you can get a healthier meal that still tastes great

2. You can cook a wide variety of foods in the air fryer so you can create lots of delicious meals and snacks

3. There are multiple types of air fryers so you can find an option that suits your needs

4. You can get air fryers of a range of shapes, sizes, and styles

5. Air fryers use less energy than a traditional convection oven and don't heat up your whole kitchen during the cooking process

6. Air fryer machines are sleek and compact, so can be left out on your kitchen countertop

7. You can move air fryers around your kitchen or store them in the cupboard if you prefer

8. Most air fryers don't require you to preheat them so you can save time in the kitchen

Are There Any Drawbacks to Using an Air Fryer?

As with any kitchen appliance, there are drawbacks to using the air fryer. There's always a cost associated with purchasing a new kitchen gadget so it might be something that you need to save up for.

You will need to learn how to use the air fryer properly before you can start cooking meals with it. Otherwise, you could have an accident and put yourself at risk. Every air fryer comes with an instruction manual so make sure you take a read through it before you start creating any delicious recipes.

Some air fryers can be quite bulky if they're large in size. You might not always be able to store them in your cupboard and they might take up a bit of space on your kitchen countertop.

Sarah Milton

However, if you know that you're going to use it often, it's worth the investment!

There's a slight risk of burning your food with an air fryer because of how close the heating elements are to the food when you're cooking. This is something to be aware of when you're following the recipes in this cookbook.

Sarah Milton

Air Fryer Recipes

Now you know everything that there is to know about air fryers, you should be equipped to find the best one for your needs. Once you've ordered one (or if you already have one), you can start browsing through the delicious recipes below!

Meat and Fish

Sarah Milton

Air Fryer Turkey Breast

MAKES 1 SERVING

PREPARATION TIME – 5 MINUTES

COOKING TIME – 10 MINUTES

NUTRITIONAL VALUES PER SERVING – 134 KCALS, 4 G CARBS, 16 G PROTEIN, 3 G FAT

Ingredients

- 1 x 100 g / 3.5 oz turkey breast steak
- 1 tsp olive oil
- 1 tsp salt

Method

1. Preheat the air fryer to 180 °C / 350 °F and line the bottom of the basket with parchment paper.
2. Coat the turkey breast steak with a light layer of olive oil. Add a little salt to the top of the steak and transfer to the air fryer. Cook for 10-12 minutes until the turkey is fully cooked and slightly golden.
3. Eat the turkey with a side of potatoes or chop it up and add it to your salads.

Air Fryer Tuna Steak

MAKES 1 SERVING
PREPARATION TIME – 5 MINUTES
COOKING TIME – 5 MINUTES
NUTRITIONAL VALUES PER SERVING – 121 KCALS, 3 G CARBS, 18 G
PROTEIN, 4 G FAT

Ingredients

- 1 x 100 g / 3.5 oz tuna steak
- 1 tsp salt

Method

1. Preheat the air fryer to 180 °C / 350 °F and line the bottom of the basket with parchment paper.
2. Sprinkle the salt over the tuna steak and place in the mesh basket. Cook for 5 minutes until the steak has darkened.
3. Serve the tuna with your favourite sauce and sides.

Tomato and Herb Chicken Breast

MAKES 1 SERVING
PREPARATION TIME – 10 MINUTES
COOKING TIME – 15 MINUTES
NUTRITIONAL VALUES PER SERVING – 145 KCALS, 5 G CARBS, 18 G
PROTEIN, 3 G FAT

Ingredients

- 1 x 100 g / 3.5 oz chicken breast fillet
- 1 tbsp tomato paste
- 1 tsp dried mixed herbs

Method

1. Preheat the air fryer to 180 °C / 350 °F and line the bottom of the basket with parchment paper.

2. Coat the chicken breast fillet with tomato paste on both sides and add a sprinkle of dried mixed herbs. Transfer to the air fryer and cook for 12-15 minutes, turning halfway through, until golden and crispy.

3. Eat the chicken breast with a side of potatoes and vegetables.

Grilled Sausages

MAKES 1 SERVING

PREPARATION TIME – 5 MINUTES

COOKING TIME – 15 MINUTES

NUTRITIONAL VALUES PER SERVING – 212 KCALS, 8 G CARBS, 16 G PROTEIN, 6 G FAT

Ingredients

- 2 x pork sausages
- 1 tsp smoked paprika
- 1 tsp black pepper

Method

1. Preheat the air fryer to 200 °C / 400 °F and line the bottom of the basket with parchment paper.
2. Place the sausages in the air fryer and sprinkle the smoked paprika and black pepper on top.
3. Close the air fryer lid and cook for 12-15 minutes until they are hot and browned.
4. Serve the sausages as part of an all-day breakfast, inside a pasta dish, or in a delicious toastie.

Chicken Nuggets

MAKES 4 SERVINGS

PREPARATION TIME – 15 MINUTES

COOKING TIME – 15 MINUTES

NUTRITIONAL VALUES PER SERVING – 278 KCALS, 10 G CARBS, 18 G PROTEIN, 7 G FAT

Ingredients

- 3 x 100 g / 3.5 oz skinless, boneless chicken breast fillets
- 2 eggs, beaten
- 1 tbsp smoked paprika
- 1 tsp garlic powder
- 1 tsp black pepper
- 100 g / 3.5 oz breadcrumbs

Method

1. Preheat the air fryer to 200 °C / 400 °F and line the bottom of the basket with parchment paper.
2. Cut the chicken breasts into small chunks.
3. In a mixing bowl, combine the eggs, smoked paprika, garlic powder, and black pepper.
4. In a separate bowl, place the breadcrumbs.
5. Dip the chicken chunks into the egg mixture, followed by the breadcrumbs. Toss to fully coat the chunks in breadcrumbs and transfer into the lined air fryer basket.
6. Cook for 12-15 minutes until crispy and golden.
7. Serve with a side of chips or veggies.

Crispy Duck

MAKES 4 SERVINGS
PREPARATION TIME – 5 MINUTES
COOKING TIME – 15 MINUTES
NUTRITIONAL VALUES PER SERVING – 170 KCALS, 7 G CARBS, 15 G
PROTEIN, 6 G FAT

Ingredients

- 2 x boneless duck breasts
- ½ tsp salt
- ½ tsp black pepper

Method

1. Preheat the air fryer to 180 °C / 350 °F and line the bottom of the basket with parchment paper.
2. Score the duck breasts using a sharp knife. Season with salt and black pepper.
3. Cook the duck breasts in the air fryer for 15 minutes until they're hot all the way through. Use a thermometer to check the internal temperature and it should be around 75 °C / 165 °F.
4. Serve with a side of plum sauce or shred and eat inside pancakes.

Turkey Burgers

MAKES 4 SERVINGS

PREPARATION TIME – 10 MINUTES

COOKING TIME – 15 MINUTES

NUTRITIONAL VALUES PER SERVING – 298 KCALS, 19 G CARBS, 22 G PROTEIN, 9 G FAT

Ingredients

- 400 g / 14 oz ground turkey
- 1 tsp chili powder
- 1 tsp ground cumin
- 1 tsp garlic powder
- 1 tsp onion powder
- 1 tbsp dried oregano
- 1 tsp black pepper
- 1 egg, beaten
- 1 tbsp sweet chili sauce

Method

1. Preheat the air fryer to 200 °C / 400 °F and line the bottom of the basket with parchment paper.

2. In a bowl, mix together the ground turkey, chili powder, ground cumin, garlic powder, onion powder, dried oregano, and black pepper in a bowl.

3. Stir in the beaten egg and sweet chili sauce until all of the ingredients are fully combined.

4. Shape the mixture into 4 even burgers and cook in the air fryer for 18-20 minutes, turning halfway through, until the meat has browned.

5. Serve the burgers in a burger bun with some fresh lettuce, tomatoes, sliced onion, and an extra squirt of sweet chili sauce.

Breaded Cod Fillets

MAKES 4 SERVINGS
PREPARATION TIME – 10 MINUTES
COOKING TIME – 10 MINUTES
NUTRITIONAL VALUES PER SERVING – 322 KCALS, 9 G CARBS, 29 G
PROTEIN, 3 G FAT

Ingredients

- 4 x 100 g / 3.5 oz cod fillets
- 4 tbsp butter, melted
- 4 garlic cloves, peeled and minced
- ½ tsp salt

Method

1. Preheat your air fryer to 180 °C / 350 °F and line the bottom of the basket with parchment paper.
2. Lay the cod fillets out on a clean surface.
3. Mix together the butter, garlic cloves, and salt. Spoon the garlic butter mixture evenly across the top of each fillet and gently press down so the filling doesn't fall off when you transfer the fillets to the air fryer.
4. Place the cod into the lined air fryer basket and cook for 10 minutes until the fish is cooked. The fillets should fall apart when you break them using a fork.
5. Serve with some lemon and dill sauce, and a side of brown rice and veggies.

Roast Pork

MAKES 4 SERVINGS

PREPARATION TIME – 20 MINUTES

COOKING TIME – 15 MINUTES

NUTRITIONAL VALUES PER SERVING – 421 KCALS, 10 G CARBS, 23 G PROTEIN, 11 G FAT

Ingredients

- 1 large pork loin
- 1 tsp salt
- 1 tsp black pepper

Method

1. Score the pork loin using a sharp knife and pat dry with a paper towel.
2. Season the pork with salt and black pepper, and refrigerate for 20 minutes.
3. Preheat the air fryer to 200 °C / 400 °F and line the bottom of the basket with parchment paper.
4. Transfer the pork loin into the air fryer with the skin side facing up. Cook for 15 minutes until golden and hot all the way through.
5. Allow the pork to cool for around 15 minutes before cutting into slices and serving.

Air Fryer Pigs in Blankets

MAKES 4 SERVINGS
PREPARATION TIME – 10 MINUTES
COOKING TIME – 10 MINUTES
NUTRITIONAL VALUES PER SERVING – 89 KCALS, 5 G CARBS, 4 G
PROTEIN, 5 G FAT

Ingredients

- 16 cocktail sausages
- 8 strips streaky bacon
- 1 tbsp olive oil

Method

1. Preheat the air fryer to 180 °C / 350 °F and line the bottom of the basket with parchment paper.
2. Cut the bacon slices in half.
3. Wrap the 16 cocktail sausages in the streaky bacon slices.
4. Brush the sausages and bacon with olive oil and transfer to the air fryer. Cook for 10 minutes until the bacon is hot and crispy.

Beef Meatballs

MAKES 4 SERVINGS

PREPARATION TIME – 30 MINUTES

COOKING TIME – 15 MINUTES

NUTRITIONAL VALUES PER SERVING – 248 KCALS, 14 G CARBS, 21 G PROTEIN, 12 G FAT

Ingredients

- 100 g / 3.5 oz plain flour
- 100 g / 3.5 oz rolled oats
- 100 g / 3.5 oz wholemeal crackers
- 2 eggs, beaten
- 1 x 400 ml can evaporated milk
- 1 tsp onion powder
- 1 tsp garlic powder
- 1 tsp cayenne pepper
- 1 tsp salt
- 800 g / 28 oz ground minced beef

Method

1. Preheat the air fryer to 180 °C / 350 °F and line the bottom of the basket with parchment paper.
2. In a large mixing bowl, combine the plain flour, rolled oats, and wholemeal crackers. Stir in the beaten eggs and evaporated milk and mix well.
3. Add the onion powder, garlic powder, cayenne pepper, and salt to the bowl.
4. Fold the beef into the mixture and stir to fully combine the ingredients.
5. Use a spoon to gather small amounts of the mixture. Roll into equal balls.
6. Transfer the meatballs into the prepared air fryer basket and cook for 15 minutes until crispy and browned.
7. Serve the meatballs hot with spaghetti and tomato sauce.

Chicken Satay

MAKES 4 SERVINGS

PREPARATION TIME – 20 MINUTES

COOKING TIME – 10 MINUTES

NUTRITIONAL VALUES PER SERVING – 201 KCALS, 5 G CARBS, 18 G PROTEIN, 8 G FAT

Ingredients

- 400 g / 14 oz skinless, boneless chicken breast, cubed
- 2 tbsp soy sauce
- 2 tbsp fish sauce
- 2 tbsp hot sauce
- 1 tbsp brown sugar
- 1 tsp garlic powder
- 2 tsp ground cumin
- 50 g / 1.8 oz roasted peanuts, chopped

Method

1. Preheat the air fryer to 200 °C / 400 °F and line the bottom of the basket with parchment paper.

2. Place the chicken cubes in a bowl. In a separate bowl, whisk together the soy sauce, fish sauce, hot sauce, brown sugar, garlic powder, and ground cumin in a bowl until fully combined.

3. Pour the sauce over the chicken and toss to coat. Leave to marinate for 20 minutes.

4. Transfer the coated chicken chunks to the air fryer and cook for 10-12 minutes until slightly browned and crispy.

5. Serve the chicken satay with some noodles and stir-fried vegetables, topped with roasted peanuts.

Chicken Wings

MAKES 4 SERVINGS
PREPARATION TIME – 10 MINUTES
COOKING TIME – 20 MINUTES
NUTRITIONAL VALUES PER SERVING – 99 KCALS, 6 G CARBS, 2 G
PROTEIN, 6 G FAT

Ingredients

- 400 g / 14 oz chicken wings

- 1 tsp salt

- 1 tsp black pepper

- 4 tbsp hot sauce

- 4 tbsp olive oil

- 1 tbsp soy sauce

- 1 tsp garlic powder

- 1 tsp onion powder

Method

1. Preheat the air fryer to 200 °C / 400 °F and line the bottom of the basket with parchment paper.
2. Season the wings with salt and pepper. Place the wings in the air fryer and cook for 15 minutes.
3. While the chicken is cooking in the air fryer, mix the hot sauce, olive oil, soy sauce, garlic powder, and onion powder in a bowl. Whisk well to fully combine.
4. Remove the chicken wings from the air fryer and toss to coat in the hot sauce. Transfer to the air fryer and cook for a further 5 minutes until the sauce is hot and sticky.
5. Serve the wings while still piping hot with a side of potato wedges and a salad.

Crab Cakes

Ingredients

- 4 tbsp mayonnaise

- 1 egg, beaten

- 2 tbsp dried chives

- 2 tsp Dijon mustard

- 1 tsp salt

- 1 tsp black pepper

- 400 g / 14 oz crab meat

- 8 crackers, crushed

Method

1. In a bowl, mix the mayonnaise, beaten egg, dried chives, Dijon mustard, salt, and black pepper.
2. Fold in the crab meat and crushed crackers until they are both fully coated in the sauce.
3. Divide the mixture into 8 equal patties and refrigerate for 15 minutes.
4. Meanwhile, preheat the air fryer to 200 °C / 400 °F and line the bottom of the basket with parchment paper.
5. Transfer the crab cakes into the lined air fryer basket and cook for 15 minutes, turning halfway through.
6. Serve the crab cakes warm with a side of tartar sauce and some cooked vegetables.

Tofu and Tempeh

Crispy BBQ Tempeh

MAKES 4 SERVINGS
PREPARATION TIME – 5 MINUTES
COOKING TIME – 10 MINUTES
NUTRITIONAL VALUES PER SERVING – 198 KCALS, 12 G CARBS, 12 G
PROTEIN, 10 G FAT

Ingredients

- 1 x 400 g / 14 oz block tempeh
- 2 tbsp BBQ sauce

Method

1. Preheat the air fryer to 200 °C / 400 °F and line the bottom of the basket with parchment paper.
2. Cut the tempeh into even chunks and coat in BBQ sauce. Transfer into the air fryer basket and cook for 10 minutes until the tempeh is sticky and crispy.
3. Serve the tempeh with some fresh noodles or brown rice and vegetables.

Tomato and Herb Tofu

MAKES 4 SERVINGS
PREPARATION TIME – 5 MINUTES
COOKING TIME – 10 MINUTES
NUTRITIONAL VALUES PER SERVING – 198 KCALS, 12 G CARBS, 12 G
PROTEIN, 10 G FAT

Ingredients

- 1 x 400 g / 14 oz block extra firm tofu
- 2 tbsp tomato and herb pasta sauce
- 1 tsp black pepper

Method

1. Preheat the air fryer to 200 °C / 400 °F and line the bottom of the basket with parchment paper.
2. Cut the tofu into even chunks.
3. Mix the tomato and herb sauce and the black pepper in a bowl. Coat the tofu piece in the sauce and place in the lined air fryer basket.
4. Cook the tofu for 12-15 minutes until crispy on the edges. Serve the tofu in a stir fry or pasta dish or add it to your salad.

Tomato Quorn Fillets

MAKES 4 SERVINGS
PREPARATION TIME – 5 MINUTES
COOKING TIME – 15 MINUTES
NUTRITIONAL VALUES PER SERVING – 201 KCALS, 8 G CARBS, 14 G
PROTEIN, 5 G FAT

Ingredients

- 4 x 100 g Quorn fillets
- 4 tbsp tomato puree
- 1 tbsp dried mixed herbs

Method

1. Preheat the air fryer to 180 °C / 350 °F and line the bottom of the basket with parchment paper.
2. Lay the Quorn fillets out on a clean surface.
3. In a bowl, mix the tomato puree and dried mixed herbs. Spread the tomato mixture over the Quorn fillets and transfer to the air fryer. Cook for 12-15 minutes until golden and hot.
4. Serve the fillets with a side of chips and vegetables or chop them up to stir into a pasta dish.

Scrambled Tofu With Soy Sauce

MAKES 4 SERVINGS

PREPARATION TIME – 5 MINUTES

COOKING TIME – 10 MINUTES

NUTRITIONAL VALUES PER SERVING – 198 KCALS, 12 G CARBS, 12 G PROTEIN, 10 G FAT

Ingredients

- 1 x 400 g / 14 oz block firm tofu
- 2 tbsp soy sauce
- 1 tsp black pepper

Method

1. Preheat the air fryer to 200 °C / 400 °F and line the bottom of the basket with parchment paper.
2. Cut the tofu into even chunks and place the soy sauce in a small bowl. Toss the tofu pieces to coat in the sauce. Sprinkle some black pepper over the tofu and transfer to the air fryer.
3. Cook the tofu for 10 minutes until crispy on the edges. Once cooked, remove the tofu and use a fork to scramble.
4. Serve for lunch while hot. You can eat the scrambled tofu on toast or stir in some vegetables for a larger meal.

Sweet and Sticky Tofu

MAKES 4 SERVINGS

PREPARATION TIME – 15 MINUTES

COOKING TIME – 15 MINUTES

NUTRITIONAL VALUES PER SERVING – 301 KCALS, 9 G CARBS, 15 G PROTEIN, 7 G FAT

Ingredients

- 1 tsp onion powder

- 1 tsp garlic powder

- 3 tbsp soy sauce

- 3 tbsp sweet chili sauce

- 1 tsp hot sauce

- 1 x 400 g / 14 oz block firm tofu, cubed

- 3 tbsp corn starch

Method

1. Preheat your air fryer to 180 °C / 300 °F and line the bottom of the basket with parchment paper.
2. In a mixing bowl, combine the onion powder, garlic powder, soy sauce, sweet chili sauce, and hot sauce.
3. Toss the tofu cubes in the sauce until fully coated. Refrigerate for 20 minutes to marinate.
4. Place the corn starch in a separate bowl and coat the tofu. Transfer the tofu to the lined air fryer basket. Cook for 15 minutes until hot and crispy.
5. Serve the tofu while hot with some pasta or noodles and veggies.

EXCLUSIVE BONUS

40 Weight Loss Recipes

&

14 Days Meal Plan

Scan the QR-Code and receive
the FREE download:

Beans and Legumes

3 Bean Chili Mix

MAKES 4 SERVINGS
PREPARATION TIME – 5 MINUTES
COOKING TIME – 20 MINUTES
NUTRITIONAL VALUES PER SERVING – 212 KCALS, 17 G CARBS, 13 G PROTEIN, 7 G FAT

Ingredients

- 1 x 400 g can kidney beans, drained and rinsed
- 1 x 400 g can white beans, drained and rinsed
- 1 x 400 g can chopped tomatoes
- 1 tbsp olive oil
- 1 tsp dried mixed herbs
- 1 tsp chili powder

Method

1. Preheat the air fryer to 180 °C / 350 °F and line the bottom of the basket with parchment paper.
2. In a large mixing bowl, combine the kidney beans, white beans, chopped tomatoes, olive oil, dried mixed herbs, and chili powder. Stir until fully combined.
3. Transfer to the air fryer basket and cook for 25-30 minutes until the mixture is hot and the beans have softened.
4. Serve the chili with some fresh yoghurt and rice.

Crispy Smoked Paprika Chickpeas

MAKES 4 SERVINGS
PREPARATION TIME – 5 MINUTES
COOKING TIME – 10 MINUTES
NUTRITIONAL VALUES PER SERVING – 129 KCALS, 18 G CARBS, 14 G
PROTEIN, 6 G FAT

Ingredients

- 1 x 400 g can chickpeas, drained and rinsed
- 1 tbsp olive oil
- 1 tbsp smoked paprika
- 1 tsp cayenne pepper

Method

1. Preheat the air fryer to 190 °C / 380 °F and line the bottom of the basket with parchment paper.
2. Place the chickpeas in a bowl and sprinkle over the smoked paprika, cayenne pepper, and olive oil. Toss to fully coat the chickpeas.
3. Transfer the chickpeas to the air fryer and cook for 10-12 minutes until they're crispy and golden.
4. Serve the chickpeas as a side or snack.

Air Fryer Burritos

MAKES 4 SERVINGS
PREPARATION TIME – 5 MINUTES
COOKING TIME – 5 MINUTES
NUTRITIONAL VALUES PER SERVING – 312 KCALS, 21 G CARBS, 16 G
PROTEIN, 11 G FAT

Ingredients

- 4 tortilla wraps

- 8 tbsp cooked white rice

- 4 tbsp mozzarella cheese, grated

- 1 x 400 g can black beans, drained and rinsed

- 1 x 400 g can chopped tomatoes

- ½ onion, finely sliced

- 1 tbsp lime juice

- 1 tbsp salsa

Method

1. Preheat the air fryer to 190 °C / 380 °F and line the bottom of the basket with parchment paper.
2. Lay out the tortilla wraps and spoon 2 tbsp of cooked white rice into centre of each one alongside 1 tbsp of mozzarella cheese.
3. In a mixing bowl, combine black beans, chopped tomatoes, and sliced onions. Squeeze in a touch of lime juice and salsa.
4. Evenly spoon the mixture on top of the rice and cheese in the centre of each wrap.
5. Carefully roll the wraps up into burritos and use a cocktail stick to keep them tightly rolled up. Place them into the lined air fryer basket and cook for 5-7 minutes until hot and slightly crispy.

Crispy Air Fryer Falafel

MAKES 4 SERVINGS
PREPARATION TIME – 10 MINUTES
COOKING TIME – 15 MINUTES
NUTRITIONAL VALUES PER SERVING – 188 KCALS, 13 G CARBS, 9 G PROTEIN, 6 G FAT

Ingredients

- ½ onion, sliced
- 2 cloves garlic, peeled and sliced
- 2 tbsp fresh parsley leaves, finely chopped
- 2 tbsp fresh coriander leaves, finely chopped
- 2 x 400 g / 14 oz chickpeas, drained and rinsed
- 1 tsp dried mixed herbs
- 1 tsp smoked paprika
- 1 tsp salt
- 1 tsp black pepper
- 1 tsp baking powder

Method

1. Preheat the air fryer to 180 °C / 350 °F and line the bottom of the basket with parchment paper.

2. Add the onion, garlic cloves, fresh parsley, and fresh coriander to a food processor and pulse in 30-second intervals until all of the ingredients are fully combined. Scrape the mixture off the sides of the food processor in between each interval if necessary.

3. Add the chickpeas, dried mixed herbs, smoked paprika, salt, black pepper, and baking powder. Pulse the mixture until fully combined. Add more water if necessary. The mixture should be dry but not too crumbly and it should be easy to form into balls.

4. Use a spoon to scoop around 2 tbsp of the mixture at a time and roll the into small balls. Place the falafel balls into the lined air fryer basket.

5. Cook the falafel balls for 12-15 minutes until golden and crispy on the edges.

6. Serve the falafels hot or cold with some hummus or tahini sauce. Alternatively, add them to some wholemeal pitta bread or a wrap.

Carbohydrates

Cinnamon French Toast

MAKES 2 SERVINGS
PREPARATION TIME – 10 MINUTES
COOKING TIME – 5 MINUTES
NUTRITIONAL VALUES PER SERVING – 256 KCALS, 16 G CARBS, 5 G
PROTEIN, 5 G FAT

Ingredients

- 4 slices bread
- 4 eggs
- 200 ml milk
- 2 tbsp brown sugar
- 1 tsp ground cinnamon
- 1 tbsp honey

Method

1. Preheat your air fryer to 150 °C / 300 °F and line the bottom of the basket with parchment paper.
2. Cut each slice of bread into 2 even rectangles.
3. In a mixing bowl, whisk together the 4 eggs, milk, brown sugar, and ground cinnamon.
4. Soak the bread slices in the egg mixture until they are fully covered.
5. Place the soaked bread in the lined air fryer baskets, close the lid, and cook for 5 minutes.
6. Serve the French toast slices with a drizzle of cinnamon and a sprinkle of extra cinnamon.

Breakfast Toasties

MAKES 1 SERVING
PREPARATION TIME – 10 MINUTES
COOKING TIME – 5 MINUTES
NUTRITIONAL VALUES PER SERVING – 278 KCALS, 25 G CARBS, 12 G
PROTEIN, 10 G FAT

Ingredients

- 2 slices bread
- 1 tsp tomato sauce
- 1 fried egg
- 2 sausages, cooked
- 1 hash brown, cooked

Method

1. Preheat the air fryer to 150 °C / 300 °F and line the bottom of the basket with parchment paper.
2. Lay one slice of bread down on a clean surface and spread 1 tsp tomato sauce evenly across the top. Lay the fried egg on top.
3. Cut the sausages in half lengthways and place on top of the egg, followed by the hash brown.
4. Place the second slice of bread on top and gently press down to seal the ingredients into the sandwich.
5. Transfer the sandwich in the air fryer and cook for 5 minutes. Turn the toastie over and cook on the other side for a further 2 minutes until both sides are crispy.

BBQ Chicken Toasted Wraps

MAKES 4 SERVINGS

PREPARATION TIME – 15 MINUTES

COOKING TIME – 10 MINUTES

NUTRITIONAL VALUES PER SERVING – 256 KCALS, 18 G CARBS, 12 G PROTEIN, 6 G FAT

Ingredients

- 100 g / 3.5 oz cooked chicken breast slices

- 4 tbsp BBQ sauce

- 4 wholemeal wraps

- 4 tbsp cheddar cheese, grated

Method

1. Preheat the air fryer to 180 °C / 350 °F and line the bottom of the basket with parchment paper.
2. Place the chicken breast chunks in a small mixing bowl and add the BBQ sauce. Toss to coat the chicken in the sauce.
3. Lay the wholemeal wraps out on a clean surface and evenly spread the BBQ chicken breast chunks in the centre of each one.
4. Add 1 tbsp of cheddar cheese on top of the chicken chunks.
5. Fold the left and right sides of each wrap over to cover the filling, followed by the top and bottom to form a square.
6. Use a cocktail stick to seal the ingredients inside the wrap and place in the air fryer. Cook for 8-10 minutes until the wrap is crispy, browned, and hot.

Air Fryer Garlic Bread

MAKES 4 SERVINGS
PREPARATION TIME – 5 MINUTES
COOKING TIME – 5 MINUTES
NUTRITIONAL VALUES PER SERVING – 117 KCALS, 12 G CARBS, 3 G
PROTEIN, 8 G FAT

Ingredients

- 4 tbsp butter, softened
- 2 garlic cloves, peeled and minced
- 1 tsp dried chives
- 4 large ciabatta breads
- 2 tbsp Parmesan cheese, grated

Method

1. Preheat the air fryer to 180 °C / 350 °F and line the bottom of the basket with parchment paper.
2. Combine the butter, minced garlic cloves, and dried chives in a small mixing bowl.
3. Lay the 4 ciabatta roles on a clean surface and spread the garlic butter mixture evenly across one side of them. Top each slice with 1 tbsp grated Parmesan cheese.
4. Transfer the ciabatta slices to the air fryer. Cook for 5 minutes until the ciabatta is golden and crispy, and the cheese has melted on top.

Egg Fried Rice

MAKES 4 SERVINGS
PREPARATION TIME – 5 MINUTES
COOKING TIME – 15 MINUTES
NUTRITIONAL VALUES PER SERVING – 213 KCALS, 18 G CARBS, 9 G
PROTEIN, 6 G FAT

Ingredients

- 400 g / 14 oz cooked white rice
- 1 tbsp olive oil
- 2 eggs, scrambled

Method

1. Preheat the air fryer to 150 °C / 300 °F and line the bottom of the basket with parchment paper.
2. In a bowl, mix the cooked rice and olive oil. Toss to coat before folding in the scrambled egg.
3. Transfer the rice to the prepared air fryer basket and cook for 15 minutes. Serve with some curry, chili, or mixed vegetables.

Vegetable Rice

MAKES 4 SERVINGS
PREPARATION TIME – 5 MINUTES
COOKING TIME – 15 MINUTES
NUTRITIONAL VALUES PER SERVING – 198 KCALS, 14 G CARBS, 8 G
PROTEIN, 4 G FAT

Ingredients

- 400 g / 14 oz cooked white or brown rice
- 100 g / 3.5 oz frozen mixed vegetables
- 1 tbsp olive oil

Method

1. Preheat the air fryer to 150 °C / 300 °F and line the bottom of the basket with parchment paper.
2. Place the cooked rice in a bowl and stir in the frozen mixed vegetables.
3. Add 1 tbsp olive oil and toss to fully coat the rice. Transfer to the air fryer basket and cook for 15 minutes until the rice has softened.
4. Serve as a side to your dinner, or add some sliced chicken or tofu to make a rice bowl for lunch.

Air Fryer Naan Bread Pizzas

MAKES 2 SERVINGS
PREPARATION TIME – 5 MINUTES
COOKING TIME – 5 MINUTES
NUTRITIONAL VALUES PER SERVING – 214 KCALS, 16 G CARBS, 8 G PROTEIN, 10 G FAT

Ingredients

- 2 plain naan breads
- 2 tbsp tomato paste
- 50 g / 1.8 oz mozzarella cheese, grated
- 1 tsp dried basil

Method

1. Preheat the air fryer to 180 °C / 350 °F and line the bottom of the basket with parchment paper.
2. Spread 1 tbsp tomato paste evenly on top of each naan bread.
3. Sprinkle some grated mozzarella on top of the tomato paste and ½ tsp of dried basil on each naan.
4. Place the naan bread pizzas in the prepared air fryer basket and cook for 5 minutes until golden and the cheese has melted.
5. Serve the pizzas with a side salad for lunch or dinner.

Sarah Milton

Cinnamon Bagels

MAKES 4 SERVINGS
PREPARATION TIME – 10 MINUTES
COOKING TIME – 10 MINUTES
NUTRITIONAL VALUES PER SERVING – 180 KCALS, 18 G CARBS, 7 G
PROTEIN, 5 G FAT

Ingredients

- 400 g / 14 oz self-raising flour

- 2 tbsp granulated sugar

- 2 tsp ground cinnamon

- 8 tbsp Greek yoghurt

- 1 tbsp olive oil

- 1 egg

Method

1. Preheat the air fryer to 180 °C / 350 °F and line the bottom of the basket with parchment paper.

2. In a large mixing bowl, combine the flour, granulated sugar, and cinnamon.

3. Stir in the Greek yoghurt and olive oil. Whisk well to combine the ingredients into a smooth and sticky dough.

4. Roll the dough into 8 equal balls. Press each ball down using your palms to create patties.

5. Use your thumb to create holes in the centre of each patty to form bagels.

6. In a bowl, whisk the eggs. Use a pastry brush to lightly coat each bagel in the beaten egg.

7. Transfer to the air fryer and cook for 10 minutes until the bagels are golden.

8. Allow them to cool for 10 minutes. Serve with some cream cheese, butter, or peanut butter on top.

Sarah Milton

Crispy Pizza Bites

MAKES 4 SERVINGS

PREPARATION TIME – 5 MINUTES

COOKING TIME – 10 MINUTES

NUTRITIONAL VALUES PER SERVING – 175 KCALS, 14 G CARBS, 6 G PROTEIN, 7 G FAT

Ingredients

- 8 x frozen pizza bites
- 1 tsp dried chives
- 1 tsp black pepper

Method

1. Preheat the air fryer to 180 °C / 350 °F and line the bottom of the basket with parchment paper.
2. Place the pizza bites in the air fryer. Sprinkle some dried chives and black pepper over the top of each one.
3. Cook for 8-10 minutes until hot and the cheese has melted.
4. Serve the pizza bites as part of a buffer or as a snack.

Fruits and Vegetables

Baked Apples

MAKES 2 SERVINGS
PREPARATION TIME – 5 MINUTES
COOKING TIME – 5 MINUTES
NUTRITIONAL VALUES PER SERVING – 67 KCALS, 14 G CARBS, 1 G
PROTEIN, 1 G FAT

Ingredients

- 2 green apples
- 1 tbsp brown sugar
- 1 tsp ground cinnamon

Method

1. Preheat the air fryer to 180 °C / 350 °F and line the bottom of the basket with parchment paper.

2. Peel the apples and cut them into small chunks and place them into the mesh basket. Sprinkle the sugar and cinnamon over the top and shut the air fryer lid.

3. Cook for 5 minutes until the apples have softened. Eat as a healthy and delicious snack.

Fried Bananas

MAKES 2 SERVINGS
PREPARATION TIME – 5 MINUTES
COOKING TIME – 5 MINUTES
NUTRITIONAL VALUES PER SERVING – 97 KCALS, 19 G CARBS, 1 G
PROTEIN, 1 G FAT

Ingredients

- 2 medium bananas
- 1 tbsp brown sugar
- 1 tsp ground nutmeg

Method

1. Preheat the air fryer to 180 °C / 350 °F and line the bottom of the basket with parchment paper.
2. Peel the bananas, cut them in half lengthways, and place them into the lined mesh baskets. Sprinkle the top of each banana half with sugar and nutmeg.
3. Cook for five minutes until the bananas have softened and are golden and crispy.
4. Eat alongside some ice cream and a drizzle of toffee sauce.

Sarah Milton

Fried Aubergine

MAKES 1 SERVING

PREPARATION TIME – 5 MINUTES

COOKING TIME – 5 MINUTES

NUTRITIONAL VALUES PER SERVING – 67 KCALS, 8 G CARBS, 2 G PROTEIN, 3 G FAT

Ingredients

- 1 large aubergine
- 1 tsp black pepper
- 1 tsp olive oil

Method

1. Preheat the air fryer to 200 °C / 400 °F and line the bottom of the basket with parchment paper.
2. Cut the aubergine in half lengthways and sprinkle with black pepper and a drizzle of olive oil.
3. Place the aubergine in the air fryer basket and cook for 5 minutes. Once cooked, remove from the air fryer and serve as a side.

Air Fryer BBQ Mushrooms

MAKES 1 SERVING

PREPARATION TIME – 5 MINUTES

COOKING TIME – 5 MINUTES

NUTRITIONAL VALUES PER SERVING – 56 KCALS, 3 G CARBS, 2 G PROTEIN, 1 G FAT

Ingredients

- 100 g / 3.5 oz button mushrooms
- 2 tbsp BBQ sauce

Method

1. Preheat the air fryer to 200 °C / 400 °F and line the bottom of the basket with parchment paper.
2. Cut the mushrooms in half and coat them in BBQ sauce. Place them in the lined air fryer basket. Close the lid and cook the mushrooms for 5 minutes until slightly browned.
3. Serve up the mushrooms as a side to your main dish.

Sweet Potato Fries

MAKES 4 SERVINGS
PREPARATION TIME – 15 MINUTES
COOKING TIME – 15 MINUTES
NUTRITIONAL VALUES PER SERVING – 212 KCALS, 15 G CARBS, 6 G
PROTEIN, 6 G FAT

Ingredients

- 200 g / 7 oz sweet potato
- 1 tbsp olive oil

Method

1. Preheat the air fryer to 200 °C / 400 °F and line the bottom of the basket with parchment paper.
2. Cut the sweet potatoes into wedges and coat in olive oil. Transfer to the air fryer and cook for 12-15 minutes until crispy.
3. Serve for lunch or dinner.

Honey Roasted Carrots

MAKES 1 SERVING

PREPARATION TIME – 5 MINUTES

COOKING TIME – 5 MINUTES

NUTRITIONAL VALUES PER SERVING – 54 KCALS, 4 G CARBS, 1 G PROTEIN, 2 G FAT

Ingredients

- 100 g / 3.5 oz carrot sticks
- 1 tbsp honey

Method

1. Preheat the air fryer to 180 °C / 350 °F and line the bottom of the basket with parchment paper.
2. Coat the carrot sticks evenly in the honey and transfer to the air fryer. Cook for 5 minutes.
3. Eat the carrot sticks as a delicious, healthy snack or side.

Crispy Air Fryer Chips

MAKES 4 SERVINGS
PREPARATION TIME – 5 MINUTES
COOKING TIME – 15 MINUTES
NUTRITIONAL VALUES PER SERVING – 265 KCALS, 15 G CARBS, 4 G
PROTEIN, 12 G FAT

Ingredients

- 200 g / 7 oz frozen chips
- 1 tsp salt
- 1 tsp olive oil

Method

1. Preheat the air fryer to 200 °C / 400 °F and line the bottom of the basket with parchment paper.
2. Place the chips in the air fryer basket and sprinkle with salt and olive oil. Cook for 15 minutes until crispy, turning halfway through.
3. Serve the chips alongside some seasoned meat or tofu.

Crispy Onion Rings

MAKES 8 SERVINGS
PREPARATION TIME – 15 MINUTES
COOKING TIME – 15 MINUTES
NUTRITIONAL VALUES PER SERVING – 188 KCALS, 12 G CARBS, 5 G
PROTEIN, 8 G FAT

Ingredients

- 2 large onions

- 200 g / 7 oz plain flour

- 2 eggs, beaten

- 2 tbsp milk

- 100 g / 3.5 oz breadcrumbs

- ½ tsp onion powder

- ½ tsp garlic powder

- 1 tsp salt

- 1 tsp black pepper

Method

1. Preheat the air fryer to 200 °C / 400 °F and line the bottom of the basket with parchment paper.
2. Peel the onions and cut them into thick rings. Separate the rings and set aside.
3. Get three clean bowls. In one, place the beaten eggs. In the next bowl, add the breadcrumbs. In the final bowl, place the spices, salt, and pepper.
4. Coat the onion rings first in the eggs, then the breadcrumbs, and finally in the spices. Make sure they are completely coated in breadcrumbs by the end of this step.
5. Transfer the onion rings to the lined mesh basket in the air fryer and cook for 10 minutes until golden and crispy.
6. Serve the onion rings as a side with your main meal.

Creamy Air Fryer Mash

MAKES 8 SERVINGS
PREPARATION TIME – 10 MINUTES
COOKING TIME – 20 MINUTES
NUTRITIONAL VALUES PER SERVING – 212 KCALS, 17 G CARBS, 4 G
PROTEIN, 9 G FAT

Ingredients

- 2 large potatoes, peeled
- 2 tbsp butter
- 1 tbsp olive oil
- 1 tsp black pepper
- 2 tsp dried chopped chives

Method

1. Preheat the air fryer to 180 °C / 350 °F and line the bottom of the basket with parchment paper.
2. Chop the potatoes into small chunks and add to the air fryer basket. Cook for 20 minutes until soft.
3. Remove the potatoes from the air fryer and use a fork or masher to mash them up into a smooth mixture.
4. Stir the butter, olive oil, black pepper, and dried chives into the mash and mix well.
5. Serve as a side with some meat, tofu, or tempeh and vegetables.

Sarah Milton

Hot and Spicy Cauliflower

MAKES 8 SERVINGS
PREPARATION TIME – 10 MINUTES
COOKING TIME – 10 MINUTES
NUTRITIONAL VALUES PER SERVING – 100 KCALS, 10 G CARBS, 3 G
PROTEIN, 4 G FAT

Ingredients

- 1 head cauliflower, broken into florets

- 2 tbsp olive oil

- 2 tbsp hot sauce

- 100 g / 3.5 oz plain flour

- 1 tsp oregano

- 1 tsp smoked paprika

- 1 tsp chili powder

- 1 tsp garlic powder

Method

1. Preheat the air fryer to 180 °C / 350 °F and line the bottom of the basket with parchment paper.
2. Place the cauliflower florets in a bowl and drizzle the olive oil and hot sauce over the top. Toss to fully coat all of the florets.
3. In a separate bowl, combine the plain flour, oregano, smoked paprika, chili powder, and garlic powder. Stir the mixture into the cauliflower and toss to coat.
4. Transfer the cauliflower to the air fryer basket and cook for 10 minutes until hot and crispy.
5. Eat the cauliflower while hot.

Sarah Milton

Air Fryer Peppers

MAKES 4 SERVINGS
PREPARATION TIME – 10 MINUTES
COOKING TIME – 15 MINUTES
NUTRITIONAL VALUES PER SERVING – 41 KCALS, 8 G CARBS, 2 G
PROTEIN, 1 G FAT

Ingredients

- 1 red bell pepper
- 1 tbsp olive oil

Method

1. Preheat the air fryer to 180 °C / 350 °F and line the bottom of the basket with parchment paper.
2. Cut the bell pepper in half and remove the seeds. Slice the pepper into long chunks and place in the lined air fryer basket.
3. Drizzle 1 tbsp olive oil over the peppers, shut the air fryer lid, and cook for 15 minutes until the peppers are crispy and slightly browned.
4. Serve the peppers as a side dish to your main meal.

Crispy Kale

MAKES 4 SERVINGS

PREPARATION TIME – 10 MINUTES

COOKING TIME – 15 MINUTES

NUTRITIONAL VALUES PER SERVING – 22 KCALS, 4 G CARBS, 1 G PROTEIN, 0 G FAT

Ingredients

- 100 g / 3.5 oz fresh kale
- 1 tsp salt
- 1 tsp black pepper

Method

1. Preheat the air fryer to 200 °C / 400 °F and line the bottom of the basket with parchment paper.
2. Chop the fresh kale into small, 1 inch chunks and sprinkle salt and black pepper over the top. Place in the air fryer and cook for 15 minutes until the kale turns dry and crispy. Serve as a snack or side.

Cheese Coated Cauliflower

MAKES 4 SERVINGS

PREPARATION TIME – 10 MINUTES

COOKING TIME – 5 MINUTES

NUTRITIONAL VALUES PER SERVING – 87 KCALS, 3 G CARBS, 3 G PROTEIN, 4 G FAT

Ingredients

- 1 large cauliflower, broken into florets

- 4 tbsp soft cheese

- 1 tsp black pepper

- 50 g / 3.5 oz cheddar or mozzarella cheese, grated

Method

1. Preheat the air fryer to 150 °C / 300 °F and line the mesh basket with parchment paper or lightly grease it with olive oil.

2. Wash and drain the cauliflower florets and place them in a bowl. Stir in the soft cheese and add a sprinkle of black pepper.

3. Toss to coat the cauliflower in the soft cheese and transfer to the lined air fryer basket. Top with the grated cheddar or mozzarella cheese to form an even layer over the cauliflower.

4. Close the lid of the air fryer and cook the cauliflower for 5 minutes until it has softened and the cheese has melted on top. If you would prefer the cheese to be crispy, cook for a further few minutes to bake the cheese.

5. Serve the cheesy cauliflower as a side dish with your dinner.

Snacks

Chocolate Bark

MAKES 8 SERVINGS

PREPARATION TIME – 10 MINUTES

COOKING TIME – 5 MINUTES

NUTRITIONAL VALUES PER SERVING – 112 KCALS, 12 G CARBS, 3 G PROTEIN, 6 G FAT

Ingredients

- 10 squares of milk chocolate, melted
- 1 tbsp chopped nuts
- 1 tbsp mixed dried fruit (raisins, sultanas, dried apricots)

Method

1. Preheat the air fryer to 180 °C / 350 °F.
2. Remove the mesh basket from the air fryer and line the bottom with parchment paper.
3. In a bowl, mix the melted chocolate, chopped nuts, and dried fruit. Pour into the lined mesh basket.
4. Transfer the mesh basket to the air fryer and cook for 3 to 5 minutes. Remove the chocolate from the air fryer and leave two sets in the freezer.

Sarah Milton

Easy Banana Protein Pancakes

MAKES 2 SERVINGS
PREPARATION TIME – 5 MINUTES
COOKING TIME – 20 MINUTES
NUTRITIONAL VALUES PER SERVING – 110 KCALS, 10 G CARBS, 10 G
PROTEIN, 3 G FAT

Ingredients

- 2 bananas
- 2 eggs, beaten
- 1 scoop vanilla protein powder

Method

1. Preheat the air fryer to 180 °C / 350 °F and line the bottom of the basket with parchment paper.
2. Peel the bananas and mash them in a bowl using a fork.
3. Whisk the eggs into the bowl and pour half of the batter into the lined air fryer basket.
4. Allow the batter to spread into a pancake shape across the bottom of the machine and cook for 10 minutes until golden and crispy.
5. Carefully remove the pancake and set aside while you cook the other pancake. Pour the remaining half of the batter into the air fryer while it's still hot and cook for 10 minutes.
6. Serve the two pancakes with some fresh fruit and honey.

Raspberry Jam Donuts

MAKES 4 SERVINGS

PREPARATION TIME – 1 HOUR 20 MINUTES

COOKING TIME – 10 MINUTES

NUTRITIONAL VALUES PER SERVING – 356 KCALS, 37 G CARBS, 12 G PROTEIN, 18 G FAT

Ingredients

- 200 ml milk

- 100 g / 7 oz granulated sugar

- 1 tbsp active dry yeast

- 1 tbsp olive oil

- 4 tbsp butter, melted

- 1 egg, beaten

- 2 tsp vanilla extract

- 400 g / 14 oz plain flour

- 4 tbsp raspberry jam

Method

1. In a large mixing bowl, whisk together the milk, granulated sugars, and active dry yeast in a bowl. Set aside to allow the yeast to get foam slightly.

2. Stir 1 tbsp olive oil and 4 tbsp melted butter into the bowl, followed by the beaten egg and vanilla extract. Mix well to combine all of the ingredients.

3. Fold in the plain flour until a smooth mixture forms.

4. Lightly flour a clean kitchen top surface and roll the dough out. Knead for a few minutes until it becomes soft and sticky.

5. Transfer the dough into a large bowl and cover it with a clean tea towel or some clean tinfoil. Leave to rise for one hour in a warm place.

6. After one hour has passed, roll out the dough on a clean floured surface. Use a rolling pin to roll the dough into a one-inch thick circle.

7. Using a round cookie cutter, shape the dough into four equal circular donuts.

8. Use a spoon to scoop 1 tbsp of raspberry jam into the centre of each donut.

9. Transfer the donuts over to the prepared air fryer basket with the raspberry jam side facing up. Make sure they aren't touching inside the air fryer.

10. Turn the air fryer on at a temperature of 150 °C / 300 °F and close the lid.
11. Cook the donuts for 8-10 minutes until slightly golden.
12. Enjoy the donuts hot or cold with an extra spoon of jam or some whipped cream. Store any leftovers in the fridge.

Lemon and Chia Muffins

MAKES 8 SERVINGS

PREPARATION TIME – 10 MINUTES

COOKING TIME – 30 MINUTES

NUTRITIONAL VALUES PER SERVING – 154 KCALS, 11 G CARBS, 6 G PROTEIN, 9 G FAT

Ingredients

- 200 g / 7 oz plain flour

- 1 tsp baking powder

- 50 g / 3.5 oz granulated sugar

- 50 g / 3.5 oz brown sugar

- 1 tsp ground cinnamon

- Peel and zest 1 lemon

- 4 tbsp chia seeds

- 2 eggs, beaten

- 100 ml milk

- 1 tsp vanilla extract

Method

1. Preheat the air fryer to 150 °C / 300 °F and line a muffin tin with cases.

2. In a large mixing bowl, combine the plain flour, baking powder, granulated sugar, brown sugar, ground cinnamon, lemon peel and zest, and chia seeds.

3. Whisk in the beaten eggs, milk, and vanilla extract. Fold in the dry ingredients and mix well.

4. Pour the batter evenly into the prepared muffin pans and transfer to the air fryer basket. Cook for 30 minutes until the muffins are golden and cooked all the way through. Insert a sharp knife into the centre of the cake. It should come out dry when the muffins are fully cooked.

5. Remove the baking tray from the air fryer and set aside to cool on a drying rack. Once fully cooled, remove the muffins from the cases and store in an airtight bread tin.

6. Serve the muffins hot or cold.

Chocolate and Blueberry Pop Tarts

MAKES 8 SERVINGS
PREPARATION TIME – 15 MINUTES
COOKING TIME – 10 MINUTES
NUTRITIONAL VALUES PER SERVING – 232 KCALS, 28 G CARBS, 5 G
PROTEIN, 13 G FAT

Ingredients

For the filling:

- 50 g / 1.8 oz fresh blueberries

- 50 g / 1.8 oz chocolate chips

- 100 g / 3.5 oz granulated sugar

- 50 g / 1.8 oz granulated sugar

- 1 tsp corn starch

For the pastry:

- 1 sheet puff pastry

For the frosting:

- 4 tbsp powdered sugar

- 1 tbsp maple syrup

Method

1. Preheat the air fryer to 180 °C / 350 °F and line the mesh basket with parchment paper or grease it with olive oil.

2. Make the filling by combining the blueberries, chocolate chips, granulated sugar, and brown sugar in a saucepan over medium heat. Stir until the mixture starts to boil before lowering the temperature. Heat through until it forms a smooth consistent mixture.

3. Whisk in the corn starch and simmer for 2 minutes. Remove the saucepan from the heat and set aside to cool.

4. Meanwhile, prepare the pastry. Roll out the large sheet of puff pastry and cut it into 8 equal rectangles.

5. Spoon 2 tbsp of the cooled blueberry and chocolate filling onto one side of each rectangle. Fold over the other side of each puff pastry rectangle to cover the filling. Press the sides down with a fork or use your fingers to seal the filling into the pastry.

6. Carefully place puff pastry rectangles into the prepared air fryer basket and cook for 10-12 minutes until the pastry is golden and crispy on all sides.

7. While the puff pastry pop tarts are cooking, make the frosting by combining the powdered sugar and maple syrup in a bowl.

8. When the puff pastry sheets are cool, spread a layer of frosting on one side of each pop tart. Allow the frosting to set before serving.
9. Store the leftover pop tarts in the fridge.

Vanilla Cheesecake

MAKES 8 SERVINGS
PREPARATION TIME – 1 HOUR 10 MINUTES
COOKING TIME – NONE
NUTRITIONAL VALUES PER SERVING – 364 KCALS, 18 G CARBS, 7 G
PROTEIN, 14 G FAT

Ingredients

For the base:

- 200 g / 7 oz cracker or digestive biscuits

- 4 tbsp butter, melted

- 2 tbsp brown sugar

For the cheesecake:

- 400 g / 14 oz cream cheese

- 200 g / 7 oz granulated sugar

- 2 tbsp plain flour

- 4 tbsp sour cream

- 1 tsp vanilla extract

- 2 eggs, beaten

Method

1. Preheat the air fryer to 150 °C / 300 °F and line a loaf tin with greaseproof paper.
2. In a bowl, combine the crackers or biscuits, melted butter, and brown sugar. Mix until the cracker or biscuit crumbs are moist
3. Transfer the crumbs to the prepared loaf tin and lightly press into the bottom to form an even base.
4. Bake the crust in the air fryer for 10 minutes.
5. Remove the crust from the air fryer and set aside to cool while you prepare the filling. Leave the air fryer running on the same temperature setting.
6. In a large mixing bowl, whisk together the cream cheese, granulated sugar, plain flour, sour cream, vanilla extract until they form a smooth mixture.
7. Fold in the eggs, one at a time.
8. Spoon the wet mixture onto the top of the baked crust. Use the back of a spoon or spatula to even out the top of the cheesecake.
9. Transfer the cheesecake back to the air fryer and cook for 20 minutes.
10. Remove the cheesecake from the air fryer and store it in the fridge overnight to set. Serve cold with a side of ice cream or whipped cream.

Delicious S'mores

MAKES 4 SERVINGS
PREPARATION TIME – 1 HOUR 10 MINUTES
COOKING TIME – 10 MINUTES
NUTRITIONAL VALUES PER SERVING – 194 KCALS, 16 G CARBS, 9 G
PROTEIN, 12 G FAT

Ingredients

- 200 g / 7 oz cracker or digestive biscuits
- Handful marshmallows
- 2 tbsp butter, melted

Method

1. Preheat the air fryer to 200 °C / 400 °F and line a loaf tin with greaseproof paper.
2. Place the crackers or biscuits in a bowl and use your hands or the back of a spoon to crush them. Continue until they resemble fine breadcrumbs.
3. Stir in the marshmallows, followed by the melted butter. Mix well to fully combine the ingredients.
4. Transfer the mixture into the lined loaf tin and cook in the air fryer for 10 minutes until the marshmallows begin to turn crispy.
5. Serve the s'mores while hot for dessert or as a delicious snack.

Basic Sponge Cake

MAKES 8 SERVINGS

PREPARATION TIME – 30 MINUTES

COOKING TIME – 30 MINUTES

NUTRITIONAL VALUES PER SERVING – 213 KCALS, 15 G CARBS, 5 G PROTEIN, 10 G FAT

Ingredients

- 100 g / 3.5 oz butter, melted
- 100 g / 3.5 oz caster sugar
- 200 g / 7 oz self-raising flour
- ½ tsp baking powder
- 2 eggs, beaten
- 2 tbsp milk
- 1 tsp vanilla extract

Method

1. Preheat the air fryer to 180 °C / 350 °F and line a loaf tin with greaseproof paper.
2. In the mixing bowl, combine the butter and caster sugar until it forms a light, fluffy mixture. Fold in the self-raising flour and baking powder.
3. Whisk in the eggs, milk, and vanilla extract until smooth.
4. Pour the cake batter into the prepared loaf tin and place the loaf tin in the air fryer. Cook for 30 minutes until the cake is golden on top and cooked all the way through. Insert a sharp knife into the centre of the cake and if it comes out dry, the cake is ready.
5. Remove the cake from the loaf tin and leave to cool on a rack. Once cooled, cut into slices and serve with some cream, jam, or chocolate sauce on top.

Cut and serve or decorate with buttercream icing or chocolate frosting.

a slice of cake on a plate.

Chocolate Chip Cookies

MAKES 8 SERVINGS
PREPARATION TIME – 15 MINUTES
COOKING TIME – 10 MINUTES
NUTRITIONAL VALUES PER SERVING – 186 KCALS, 12 G CARBS, 3 G
PROTEIN, 5 G FAT

Ingredients

- 100 g / 3.5 oz butter, melted

- 50 g / 1.8 oz granulated sugar

- 50 g / 1.8 oz brown sugar

- 1 egg, beaten

- 1 tsp vanilla extract

- 200 g / 7 oz plain flour

- 100 g / 3.5 oz milk chocolate chips

- 1 tsp baking powder

- ½ tsp salt

Method

1. Preheat the air fryer to 180 °C / 350 °F and line a tray with greaseproof paper.
2. In a bowl, mix the melted butter, granulated sugar, and brown sugar until fully combined.
3. Whisk in the beaten egg and vanilla extract.
4. Fold in the plain flour, milk chocolate chips, baking powder, and salt.
5. Split the dough into 8 equal balls and flatten into cookies that are around 1 inch thick.
6. Place the cookies on the lined baking tray and cook in the air fryer for 10 minutes until golden.
7. Allow the cookies to cool on a drying rack.

Sarah Milton

Double Chocolate Brownies

MAKES 8 SERVINGS
PREPARATION TIME – 15 MINUTES
COOKING TIME – 10 MINUTES
NUTRITIONAL VALUES PER SERVING – 197 KCALS, 13 G CARBS, 5 G
PROTEIN, 7 G FAT

Ingredients

- 100 g / 3.5 oz butter, melted

- 100 g / 2.5 oz granulated sugar

- 1 egg, beaten

- 100 ml milk (any kind)

- 1 tsp vanilla extract

- 200 g / 7 oz plain flour

- 1 tsp baking powder

- 2 tbsp cocoa powder

- 100 g / 3.5 oz milk chocolate chips

- ½ tsp salt

Method

1. Preheat the air fryer to 180 °C / 350 °F and line a baking tin with greaseproof paper.
2. In a bowl, mix the melted butter and granulated sugar until fluffy.
3. Whisk in the beaten egg, milk, and vanilla extract until fully combined.
4. In a separate bowl, combine the flour, baking powder, cocoa powder, milk chocolate chips, and salt.
5. Fold the dry ingredients into the wet mixture and mix well. Pour the batter into the lined baking tin.
6. Cook in the air fryer for 15 minutes until set on the top but still slightly soft in the middle.
7. Remove the brownies from the air fryer and set aside to cool before slicing and serving.
8. Eat the brownies hot or cold with some ice cream or whipped cream.

Sarah Milton

Triple Chocolate Lava Cake

MAKES 8 SERVINGS

PREPARATION TIME – 10 MINUTES

COOKING TIME – 15 MINUTES

NUTRITIONAL VALUES PER SERVING – 401 KCALS, 21 G CARBS, 8 G PROTEIN, 14 G FAT

Ingredients

- 50 g / 3.5 oz dark chocolate chips

- 50 g / 3.5 oz milk chocolate chips

- 50 g / 3.5 oz white chocolate chips

- 100 g / 3.5 oz butter, cubed

- 100 g / 3.5 oz granulated sugar

- 3 eggs, beaten

- 1 tsp vanilla extract

- 100 g / 3.5 oz plain flour

Method

1. Preheat your air fryer to 180 °C / 350 °F and line a loaf tin with greaseproof paper.

2. In a bowl, mix the dark, milk, and white chocolate chips, and butter in a large heatproof bowl and heat in the microwave in 30 second intervals until fully melted. Stir well in between intervals to avoid the chocolate from clumping together.

3. Stir in the granulated sugar, beaten eggs, and vanilla extract.

4. Fold in the flour and mix until all of the ingredients are fully combined into one smooth mixture.

5. Transfer the cake batter into the prepared loaf tin and cook in the air fryer for 15 minutes until the cake is set on the outside but still soft in the centre. Insert a knife into the centre of the cake and it should come out mostly dry when the cake is cooked.

6. Remove the cake from the air fryer and set aside to cool on a rack for 10 minutes before cutting into slices.

7. Serve the lava cake hot or cold with a scoop of ice cream or a squirt of whipped cream.

EXCLUSIVE BONUS

40 Weight Loss Recipes

&

14 Days Meal Plan

Scan the QR-Code and receive
the FREE download:

Disclaimer

This book contains opinions and ideas of the author and is meant to teach the reader informative and helpful knowledge while due care should be taken by the user in the application of the information provided. The instructions and strategies are possibly not right for every reader and there is no guarantee that they work for everyone. Using this book and implementing the information/recipes therein contained is explicitly your own responsibility and risk. This work with all its contents, does not guarantee correctness, completion, quality or correctness of the provided information. Misinformation or misprints cannot be completely eliminated.

Printed in Great Britain
by Amazon

85539069R00064